D0186014

LEABHARLANNA CHONTAE NA GAILLIMHE
(GALWAY COUNTY LIBRARIES)

GALWAY COUNTY LIBRARIES

WITHDRAWN FROM CIRCULATION

A Giant Tree
in the Rainforest

First published in the UK in 2000 by
Belitha Press Limited
London House, Great Eastern Wharf,
Parkgate Road, London SW11 4NQ

Copyright © Belitha Press Limited 2000
Text copyright © Sally Morgan 2000
Illustrations by James Field

Editor: Russell McLean
Designer: Louise Morley
Picture researcher: Sally Morgan
Educational consultant: Emma Harvey

All rights reserved. No part of this book may be reproduced or
utilized in any form or by any means, electronic or mechanical,
including photocopying, recording or by any information storage
and retrieval system, without permission in writing from the publisher,
except by a reviewer who may quote brief passages in review.

ISBN 1 84138 170 5

Printed in Singapore

British Library Cataloguing in Publication Data
for this book is available from the British Library.

10 9 8 7 6 5 4 3 2 1

Picture acknowledgements:
Andrew Brown/Ecoscene: i4t, 23. Anthony Cooper/Ecoscene:
front cover cl, 7b, 9c. Joel Creed/Ecoscene: 29bl. Ecoscene:
cover background, 6, 27. Thomas Ennis/Ecoscene: 7c. Simon Grove/
Ecoscene: 28b. Alexandra Jones/Ecoscene: 13. Wayne Lawlor/Ecoscene:
15bl, 24c, 25t. Guy Marks/Sylvia Cordaiy Photo Library: 22b.
Sally Morgan/Ecoscene: 10, 28-29. Papilio: front cover cl, 11cr, 12-13t,
14b, 18b, 21c, 26b. Ken Preston-Mafham/Premaphotos: 9br, 12b, 15r,
17b, 18t, 19, 19br, 21t, 23t, 24-25, 26t. Nick Rains/Sylvia Cordaiy
Photo Library: 3, 20. Barrie Watts: front cover tl & br, 7t, 9t, 10c,
11l, 16b, 16-17, 17t, 21b, 22t, 25b.

Words in **bold** are explained in the glossary on page 30.

J115 974
£9.99

GALWAY COUNTY LIBRARIES

Life in ...

A Giant Tree in the Rainforest

Sally Morgan

Belitha Press

Contents

What is a rainforest?   6

Rainforest layers   8

Inside the rainforest   10

The roof   12

Plant life   14

Animals of the canopy   16

Finding food   18

The hunters   20

The dark floor   22

Recycling the waste   24

New life   26

Saving the rainforests   28

Glossary   30

Index   32

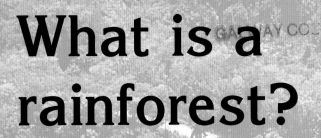

What is a rainforest?

GALWAY COUNTY LIBRARIES

A rainforest is a thick forest where tall trees grow close together. Rainforests are found in the **tropical** parts of the world near the **Equator**. The **climate** is hot and wet all year round.

There may be as many as ten million different types of plants and animals living on Earth. Rainforests are home to two-thirds of them. Some animals live among the leaves of the trees. Other animals live on the tree trunks or the forest floor. A tiny area of rainforest can contain thousands of different plants. There may be hundreds of different insects living on one giant tree. We say that the rainforests have a high **biodiversity**. This means there is a great variety of plants and animals living there.

▲ The trees in a rainforest grow very close together. The forest spreads for hundreds of kilometres.

▲ Macaws visit this river bank in the forest to lick salt.

▶ The flowers of the giant tree are brightly coloured to attract insects, birds and bats.

Rainforest layers

The rainforest has many floors, or layers, just like a tall building. Each floor is home to a different group of plants and animals.

The top layer is made up of the leaves and branches of the trees. It is called the **canopy**. The trees grow to heights of 40 metres or more. A few tall trees rise up above the others. These are **emergent trees**. Most of the animals of the rainforest live in the canopy. Colourful birds fly around the top of the trees, while monkeys and sloths move through the branches.

The next layer is the **understorey**. It is much darker here, because the canopy cuts out the light. Only a few **shrubs** and small trees, such as palms, can survive here. Climbing plants called **lianas** reach up from the forest floor.

The forest floor is a very gloomy, damp place. The ground is covered in leaves, twigs and fruits which fall from the trees above.

Canopy
The leaves and branches of trees form the canopy.

Understorey
Little light penetrates the canopy. Palms and tree ferns grow in the gloomy conditions.

Floor
The forest floor is dark and damp, and covered with leaves, fallen fruit and nuts. Only plants such as mosses and ferns can live here.

Inside the rainforest

It rains almost every day in a tropical rainforest. The air is hot and steamy. Rainwater drips off leaves and runs down tree trunks. The forest soaks up much of the water, just like a sponge.

Every morning, mist and low clouds hang over the forest. The forest floor is muddy and criss-crossed by small streams. When the sun comes out, the leaves of the giant tree stop much of the sunlight from reaching the ground. Animals cannot see each other easily in the gloom. They make a lot of noise to tell each other where they are. The rainforest is full of the sounds of croaking frogs, chirping cicadas and chattering monkeys.

When it rains on the giant tree, water runs down the trunk and drips off the leaves on to the forest floor (right). The roots of the tree take up some of the water. The rest drains into streams. When the sun comes out, the temperature rises quickly. Water **evaporates** from the leaves. It turns into a gas, or vapour. The water vapour rises into the air, where it cools and **condenses** back into water droplets. The droplets fall back to the forest as rain.

▲ The cicada makes all sorts of sounds – from quiet buzzing to a noise like a chainsaw.

◀ The howler monkey is one of the noisiest animals in the forest.

The roof

The leaves of the giant tree form a green roof, or **canopy**, over the rest of the forest. Above the forest it is bright and windy. The tree shelters smaller plants from the wind and the tropical sun.

▼ The top of the canopy is home to many birds.

The giant tree uses its leaves to make food from sunlight. This is called **photosynthesis**. To trap as much light as possible the tree has many leaves. They are arranged so they do not overlap each other. Plant leaves are green because they contain a substance called **chlorophyll**. This is essential for photosynthesis.

◄ Above the canopy it is bright and windy. Below the canopy it is gloomy and the air is still.

12

sunlight

oxygen

water

sugar

carbon dioxide

During the day, the chlorophyll in the leaves **absorbs** light energy from the sun. This energy is used to turn **carbon dioxide** gas from the air and water from the soil into sugar. The tree uses the sugar to grow. Photosynthesis also produces a gas called **oxygen**. This is released into the air. Oxygen is needed by most animals, as well as plants, to survive.

Plant life

Many smaller plants live on the giant tree. Hanging plants called **epiphytes** grow on the branches and trunk. **Lianas** climb from the forest floor to the canopy. Some plants even feed on insects.

▲ Epiphytes do not harm the tree they grow on. Their roots dangle in the air and absorb moisture.

◄ Pools of water often form in the leaves of bromeliad plants. Frogs may lay their eggs here.

Ferns, orchids and bromeliads are all epiphytes. They anchor themselves to the branches of the giant tree. This means they get more light than they would on the forest floor.

Lianas are climbing plants. They start life on the ground. Then their long stems grow up the tree towards the canopy.

Some plants eat insects. Their sticky leaves snap shut around any insect that lands on them. The pitcher plant has jug-shaped leaves. Water collects in the jug. An insect which falls into the jug drowns. Its body is broken down to make **nutrients**, or food, for the plant.

▶ The stems of lianas are like ropes. Animals use them to move up and down the tree.

▲ The leaves of the pitcher plant contain small pools of water.

Animals of the canopy

The canopy is the home for most of the animals that live in the rainforest. They live in the cool shelter of the branches of the giant tree.

Monkeys, sloths and snakes use the branches of the tree to move through the forest. Birds make their nests in tree trunks and branches. The flying squirrel and the tree frog have flaps of skin between their legs, like wings. They use them to glide from tree to tree.

Where there is a gap in the branches, large and colourful butterflies flutter from flower to flower. They like to fly in the sunny spots.

◀ This three-toed sloth uses its hook-like claws to grip branches in the canopy.

Insects hide among the green leaves of the tree. Many of the insects are the same colour as the leaves, which makes them difficult to spot. This is called **camouflage**.

▼ This green parrot has made its nest in a hole in a tree trunk.

Finding food

The giant tree provides food for many of the forest animals. Plant-eating animals eat the leaves, seeds and fruits of the tree. Without the tree, these animals could not survive.

▲ Many of the leaves of the tree are full of holes made by insects.

Animals that eat plants are called **herbivores**. Insects eat the leaves of the giant tree. Larger animals, such as toucans, macaws and monkeys, eat its nuts and fruits. These animals help to scatter the tree's fruit seeds around the forest in their **dung**. One day the seeds may grow into new trees. The herbivores are eaten by meat-eating animals such as eagles, spiders and snakes. Animals that eat meat are called **carnivores**.

◀ Parrots use their strong beaks to break open the hard nuts of the giant tree.

18

▼ Leaf-cutter ants cut out tiny pieces from leaves and carry them back to their nest.

The tree needs animals to **pollinate** its flowers. When birds, bats and insects visit the flowers to drink the sugary **nectar**, they become covered in **pollen**. They carry the pollen to other flowers. This pollinates the flowers. Once a flower has been pollinated, it can produce seeds.

▲ This hummingbird is drinking nectar.

The hunters

Many of the animals in the canopy are **predators**. This means that they feed on other animals, such as the smaller herbivores. All predators are carnivores.

Eagles sit on the branches of the tallest trees, looking for animals moving in the canopy. They hunt smaller birds and monkeys by swooping down on them from above.

▶ Spiders kill other animals with their poisonous bite. This spider is eating a moth.

GALWAY COUNTY LIBRARIES

▼ Snakes often swallow other animals whole. This snake is feeding on a tree frog.

▼ Ocelots are nocturnal. This means they sleep during the day and hunt at night.

Some hunters hide among the leaves of the tree. They jump out and catch any **prey** that passes. Snakes lie still, wrapped around the branches of the tree. Cats, such as the ocelot and margay, hunt for birds, snakes and lizards among the branches. Spiders spin huge webs which trap butterflies and other flying insects. Leeches drop from the tree on to passing animals. The leeches bite through their skin and suck their blood.

J115,974

The dark floor

The forest floor beneath the giant tree is covered in fallen leaves, twigs and nuts. It is dark and very **humid**, but cooler than the canopy. It smells musty.

Only a few plants can grow on the forest floor. Ferns and mosses can survive in the gloom and the damp soil. At the base of the tree are huge wing-shaped roots. These are called **buttress roots**. They support the tree on the thin soil.

▲ The jaguar has a dark, spotted body so that it can creep up on prey without being seen.

The larger animals of the forest live on the forest floor. Deer, **peccaries** and tapirs feed on the fallen nuts and fruits. The jaguar hunts on the floor and among the branches of the canopy. Poison arrow frogs, ants and termites live among the lowest leaves of the forest.

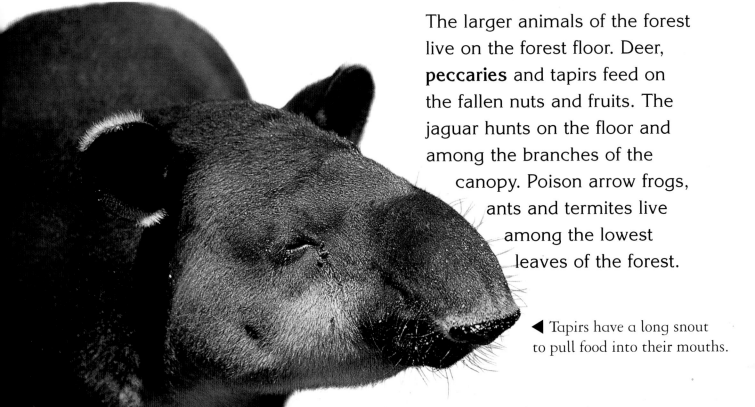

◄ Tapirs have a long snout to pull food into their mouths.

▲ Ginger plants can survive in the gloom created by the tree above.

▶ Around the buttress roots of the giant tree, the ground is covered with dead leaves and twigs.

Recycling the waste

Nothing goes to waste on the forest floor. Beetles feed on the bodies of dead animals. Termites and ants march in long columns, looking for food on the floor.

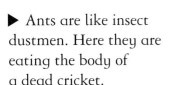

▶ Ants are like insect dustmen. Here they are eating the body of a dead cricket.

The warm and wet conditions on the forest floor are ideal for decay. Dead twigs, leaves and animals rot quickly. They are broken down within a few weeks by **fungi**, worms and **bacteria**. The dead plants and animals contain nutrients. These are released into the soil. Plants use the nutrients to grow.

▲ The tough veins of this leaf take longer to break down than the soft green part.

▲ Mushrooms are fungi. They release millions of tiny **spores** which land on the ground and grow into new fungi.

◄ Every morning, termites leave their nests to search for food on the forest floor.

New life

A giant tree can live for hundreds of years. One day it will die and topple over, or it may be blown down in a storm. When it crashes to the ground, it pulls lianas and other trees with it.

▲ This fallen tree has pulled lianas down to the forest floor.

The fallen tree makes a gap in the canopy. Light reaches the forest floor. On the ground are the seeds of the giant tree, waiting for the right conditions to grow. Now there is light, the seeds can **germinate**. The seeds grow into **saplings**.

The saplings grow as fast as they can to reach the light. It is a race for survival. Only one sapling will survive. The sapling that grows the fastest will block the light from the others. This sapling will win the race to grow into a new giant tree. The forest cycle is complete.

◀ Weevils and other insects feed on the decaying wood of the trunk.

▼ Many saplings grow
around the fallen tree,
but only one will grow
into a new giant tree.

Saving the rainforests

One hundred years ago, more than 14 per cent of the world's land surface was covered by rainforest. Now only half of the forests remain, and the rest are under threat.

Rainforest trees are being cut down to make room for houses and industry. Their wood is used to make new homes and furniture, or it is burnt as fuel. Forests are cleared to make way for crops of rubber trees and oil palms. Sometimes, the land is used as **pasture** for beef cattle.

▲ Wood from rainforest trees is used to make furniture and build houses.

The destruction of the rainforests is called **deforestation**. When forests disappear, the animals and plants that live in them disappear too. We have to **conserve** the rainforests to protect the world's biodiversity.

GALWAY COUNTY LIBRARIES

Forests can be protected by making them nature reserves or national parks. Many people want to visit rainforests to see the wildlife. Tourism can protect the rainforests by giving jobs to local people.

◀ These tourists are watching wildlife.

Glossary

absorb To soak up.

bacteria Tiny, single-celled organisms, too small to be seen with the naked eye.

biodiversity The variety of living plants and animals.

buttress roots Large, wing-like, spreading roots at the base of a tall rainforest tree.

camouflage An animal's colour and patterns which help it to blend in with the background.

canopy The highest layer of the rainforest, formed by the branches and leaves of trees.

carbon dioxide A colourless gas in the air. Animals breathe out carbon dioxide.

carnivore An animal that eats other animals.

chlorophyll A green substance in plant leaves that traps the light energy in sunlight.

climate The usual weather conditions of an area.

condense To change from a gas to a liquid – as when water vapour turns into liquid water.

conserve To look after or protect.

deforestation Cutting down or burning large areas of forests.

dung Animal droppings.

emergent trees Very tall trees that grow higher than the canopy.

epiphyte A plant that grows on the trunk or branches of a tree without doing any harm.

Equator An imaginary line around the centre of the Earth.

evaporate To change from a liquid to a gas – as when liquid water turns into water vapour.

fungi Organisms that are neither animals or plants. Most fungi are made up of tiny threads that grow through the soil.

germinate To begin to grow.

herbivore An animal that eats only plants.

humid Air which contains lots of water vapour and feels damp is humid.

liana A climbing plant that lives in rainforests.

nectar A sugary liquid produced by plants.

nutrient Chemicals that plants and animals need for healthy growth.

oxygen A colourless gas in the air. Most plants and animals need oxygen to live.

pasture Grass-covered land for cattle to graze on.

peccary A pig-like animal that lives in rainforests.

photosynthesis The way green plants make their own food using sunlight. The leaves use light energy to combine carbon dioxide and water to make sugar and oxygen. Plants use the sugar as fuel.

pollen Yellow, powdery grains produced by the stamens (the male parts) of flowers.

pollinate To take pollen from one flower to another.

predator An animal that hunts and eats other animals.

prey An animal that is hunted by other animals for food.

sapling A young tree.

shrub A small, tree-like bush.

spore A type of seed made by fungi, ferns and mosses.

tropical To do with the tropics – the hot, damp regions of the Earth near the Equator.

understorey The layer of shrubs and small trees beneath the canopy.

FURTHER READING

The following titles give more information about the plants and animals in this book. Some titles may be out of print, and only available in libraries.

Ecology Watch – Rainforests, Rodney Aldis, Cloverleaf, 1991.
Eyewitness Guides: Jungle, Theresa Greenaway, Dorling Kindersley, 1994.
Saving the Rainforests, Sally Morgan, Franklin Watts, 1999.
The Wayland Atlas of Rainforests, Anna Lewington, Wayland, 1996.
What is a Rainforest? Natural History Museum, Marshall Editions, 1989.

Index

ants 19, 22, 24

bacteria 24, 30
bats 7, 19
biodiversity 7, 29, 30
birds 7, 8, 12, 16, 17, 19,
    20, 21
branches 8, 9, 14, 15, 16,
    17, 20, 21, 22
bromeliads 14, 15
butterflies 16, 21
buttress roots 22, 23, 30

camouflage 17, 30
canopy 8, 9, 12-13, 14, 15,
    16-17, 20, 22, 26, 30
carbon dioxide 13, 30
carnivores 18, 20-21, 30
chlorophyll 12, 13, 30
cicadas 10, 11
climate 6, 30
conservation 29

decay 24
deforestation 28-29, 30
dung 18, 30

eagles 18, 20
emergent trees 8, 30
epiphytes 14, 15, 30
Equator 6, 30

ferns 9, 15, 22
flowers 7, 16, 19
food 15, 18-19, 22

forest floor 7, 8, 9, 10, 11,
    14, 15, 22-23, 24, 25, 26
frogs 10, 14, 16, 21, 22
fruits 8, 9, 18, 22
fungi 24, 25, 30

germination 26, 30

herbivores 18, 20, 30
houses 28
hunters 20-21

industry 28
insects 7, 14, 15, 17, 18,
    19, 21, 26

jaguars 22

leaves 7, 8, 9, 10, 11, 12,
    13, 15, 17, 18, 19, 21,
    22, 23, 24, 25
leeches 21
lianas 8, 14, 15, 26, 31
light 8, 9, 10, 12, 13, 15, 26

macaws 7, 18
monkeys 8, 10, 11, 16, 18, 20
mosses 9, 22

nature reserves 29
nectar 19, 31
nutrients 15, 24, 31
nuts 9, 18, 22

ocelots 21
oxygen 13, 31

palms 8, 9
parrots 17, 18
pasture 28, 31
peccaries 22, 31
photosynthesis 12, 13, 31
pitcher plants 15
pollen 19, 31
pollination 19, 31
predators 20-21, 31
prey 21, 22, 31

rain 10, 11
roots 11, 14, 22, 23

saplings 26, 27, 31
seeds 18, 19, 26
shrubs 8, 31
sloths 8, 16, 17
snakes 16, 18, 21
soil 13, 22, 24
spiders 18, 21
spores 25, 31
sun 10, 11, 12, 13

tapirs 22
termites 22, 24, 25
toucans 18
tourism 29
tree trunk 7, 10, 11, 14,
    16, 26

understorey 8, 9, 31

waste 24-25
water 10, 11, 13, 14, 15
weevils 26